The Day the Sky Turned Green

by Barbara Reeves
Illustrated by Pam Posey-Tanzey

Modern Curriculum Press

ISBN 0-7652-0880-6

Printed in the United States of America

6 7 8 9 10 11 12 13   07 06 05 04 03 02

1-800-321-3106
www.pearsonlearning.com

Contents

Chapter 1
My Name Is Champ

My name is Champ. I'm a search and rescue dog. In lots of ways, I'm like any other dog. I chase sticks and eat doggy treats. My master, Officer Fields, is my best friend.

If you saw me on the street, you would say I was a pretty nice dog. I am! But, you probably would not guess how I make my living.

I usually don't "talk" about my work. However, there is one story that really makes me proud. It happened last week. . . .

Officer Fields and I were visiting Mrs. Brown's class. We were telling the children about the rescue work we do. Well . . . Officer Fields was telling about it. I was wagging my tail to agree.

Officer Fields told the kids about my training. He told them that I went to school for five years. He explained how I can find a person by using my sense of smell.

You see, people give off a smell. The smell is really a gas that comes from skin cells that people shed. My nose is super-sensitive. That means I can smell this gas even when a person is below dirt, water, or snow. In fact, my nose is hundreds of times more powerful than Officer Fields's nose—or yours!

Mostly, Officer Fields and I are called to find missing people. Sometimes a person is just lost. Other times there might be a bad storm. I can find people who may be trapped in deep snow or buried under parts of buildings that have come down. Our work can be hard and dangerous, but we love it!

Talking to children about our work is another part of our job.

After our talk last week, Officer Fields and I handed out a special picture of ourselves. I look very good in the picture, if I do say so myself!

Most of the kids took the picture and
thanked us. A boy named Roberto stayed to
talk to us. He wanted to know all about me.
Officer Fields signed Roberto's picture. Then
he took out a special ink pad. I pressed my
paw into the pad. I "signed" the picture with
my paw print. Roberto loved it!

Before we left, Roberto asked if he could
pet me. Officer Fields said yes.

Roberto patted my head. He scratched me
behind the ears, just the way I like it. I sniffed
Roberto's "kid smell." It was like bubble gum,
paste, and gym shoes all rolled into one!

Officer Fields talked with Roberto a little longer. Then he and I headed for our car. Mrs. Brown's class had just gone outside to play. I got to bark goodbye to all the children.

As we pulled away, I saw Roberto again. I barked extra loud just for him. I really liked Roberto. I wondered if we would ever meet again.

Chapter 2
The Sky Turns Green

When we left the school, Officer Fields turned on his special radio. We heard some police calls. Then we heard a weather report. Heavy thunderstorms were moving in. Officer Fields said we should keep listening to the radio and watching the sky.

Officer Fields and I had to give one more talk that day. We were headed for a school in another county. The drive would take about an hour. I was hoping it would not rain too hard. That way I could see out the car window.

I put my nose out the window and sniffed
the air. It was spring, and wildflowers were in
bloom. I don't care much for flowers. I do like
to look for wild animals that hide nearby.

There was a time when I would have chased any wild animal. But now I am a search and rescue dog. I know I have better things to do.

Just as I sniffed a smell that had to be a fox,
a big raindrop fell on my nose. Then another
drop fell, and another. Soon the rain was
coming down hard on the roof of the car.

"Looks like we're in for a big storm, boy,"
Officer Fields said to me.

We both jumped as we heard a loud
thunderclap. Suddenly the rain turned to large
balls of hail.

Officer Fields looked in his rearview mirror. Then he let out a long, slow whistle. It was the kind of whistle he makes when things aren't so good.

I turned around and looked out the back window. The sky behind us was dark. It was filled with low-hanging clouds and was a very strange color. The sky had turned green!

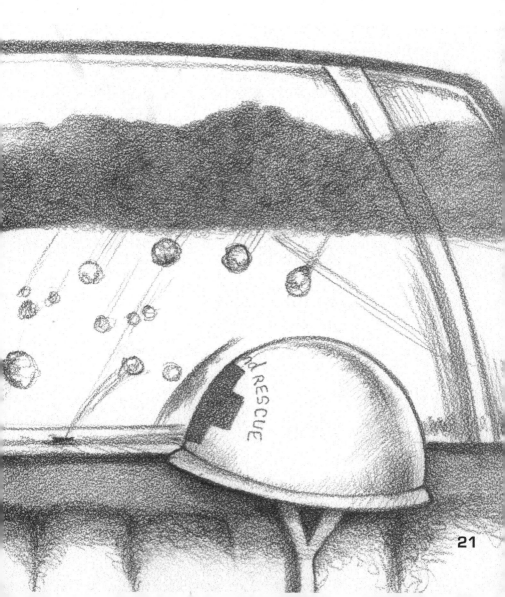

Chapter 3
Bad News

Another weather report came over the radio: "A tornado warning has been given for the following three counties. . . ."

I knew a tornado warning was serious. It meant that at least one tornado had been seen. I also knew Roberto's school was in one of the counties named! I barked very loudly to make sure Officer Fields heard the report. He put up his hand to tell me to be quiet.

"Easy, boy," Officer Fields said.

Officer Fields started to talk to himself.
"I know those kids are in good hands. The
school has held plenty of tornado drills."

Then he looked in the mirror again. A
frown spread over his face.

"We need to check on the children," Officer Fields said. He reached over to talk into the radio. Just then we heard another report.

"There is a report that a tornado has been sighted near Washington Elementary School. All emergency services should stay tuned for further instructions."

Officer Fields pulled over to the side of the road. He looked worried. He drummed his fingers on the steering wheel. Then he quickly turned the car around.

"I'm not taking any chances," he said. "Hold on boy, we're going back to the school now!"

As we drove, I looked at the sky. It wasn't green anymore. The rain and hail had stopped. The wind was still blowing. It pushed hard against the car as we moved down the road.

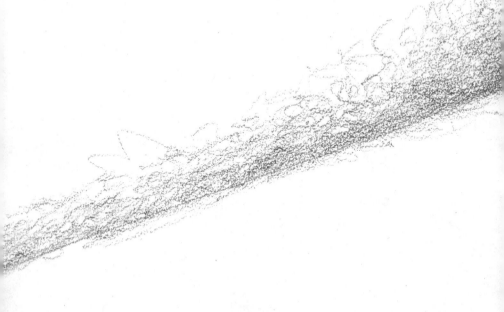

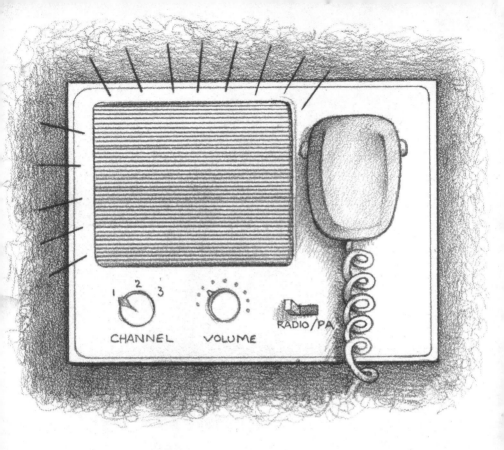

Another report came over the radio. The report started with some police codes and numbers. Then I heard the worst news. . . .

"Washington School has been hit by a tornado. Repeat, Washington School has been hit by a tornado! All emergency services report there."

Oh, no!

Chapter 4
To the Rescue

Officer Fields turned on the car's siren and lights. We blasted down the road as fast as we could.

I like going on calls. Usually I'm excited because I know I can help. This time I was worried. A tornado at an elementary school could mean plenty of trouble!

I pictured Roberto in my mind. I remembered the way he scratched me behind the ears. I remembered how much he liked my picture.

I let out a low moan. It was between a growl and a whine. I am not usually a growler or a whiner. I couldn't help myself.

Officer Fields seemed to know just what I was thinking.

"I'm worried about the kids, too," he said. "I hope they are all right."

Finally, we reached the school. Police and emergency workers were already there.

I looked around. Part of the school had been smashed by the tornado. It was the part where the classrooms were!

Officer Fields jumped out of the car. He told me to stay. I watched him talk to emergency workers.

I wanted to get out, too. I knew the children needed my help.

Officer Fields came back to the car. He opened the door.

"Champ," he said, "most of the children are safe. The teachers took them to the hallway near the gym. There aren't any windows there. The walls are strong."

Then Officer Fields took a deep breath. I knew something was wrong.

"Roberto didn't stay in the hallway. He left just before the tornado hit. His teacher said she didn't see him go."

Where was Roberto?

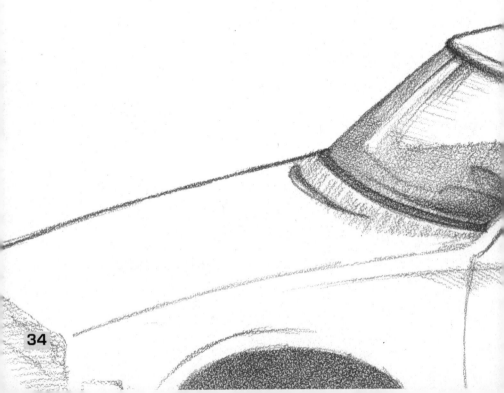

Chapter 5
After the Tornado

I stared at Officer Fields with a questioning look.

"I don't know why he left the hallway," he said. "Roberto is still missing. We need to find him."

Officer Fields opened the back door of the car. I hopped out, ready to go!

The first thing I noticed was the temperature. It had changed. The day was warm and muggy before the storm. Now it felt cool.

I sniffed the air and remembered what
Officer Fields says about tornadoes. He says
that tornadoes form when cool, dry air bumps
into warm, muggy air. The warm air rushes
upward. Then more warm air moves in to
take its place. Sometimes it only gets stormy.

Other times the air begins to move around and around. When this happens, a tornado is born.

Tornadoes are very powerful. They can move across the ground as fast as a car. Inside, winds whirl around and around. The winds spin at more than 200 miles per hour!

Tornadoes can suck large trees right out of the ground. They can carry cars through the air. They can also do damage in strange ways.

A tornado may hit only one house on a block. It may flatten a whole building or just part of the building.

You see, when a tornado goes over a building, it sucks up all the air. The air pressure outside the building becomes very low. The air pressure inside the building stays the same. This change in air pressure is dangerous. It can make a whole building, or part of it, explode outward.

Tornadoes usually happen without too much warning. That is why it is important for people to know what to do if there is the chance of a tornado.

41

Just thinking about the damage a tornado can do made me uneasy. I thought about how scared Roberto must be.

"Hold on, Roberto," I said to myself, "I'm on my way to find you!"

Chapter 6
A Good Day's Work

With Officer Fields behind me, I began my work. I sniffed around the schoolyard. There were plenty of "people smells" there!

I looked around. Parents were beginning to arrive. I couldn't see the children. They must be somewhere safe, I thought.

I moved closer to the part of the building
that had fallen. I stopped thinking about what
was around me. I only paid attention to smells.
My nose led the way.

I smelled damp wood. I smelled a funny smell that comes from walls that have crumbled.

I remembered Roberto's special smell. That helped. But I knew I could find Roberto even if I did not remember his smell. My nose never lets me down!

Suddenly, my nose picked up the smell of a person. Roberto was nearby! I barked once to let Officer Fields know I was on the trail.

I saw a large heap of wood and broken walls in front of me. My nose told me to move closer. As I did, I heard a small noise. I barked twice to tell Officer Fields to stay close.

My nose picked up more smells. Then I heard a voice calling for help.

At first the voice was tiny and quiet. Then it became louder. It was Roberto!

Officer Fields was right behind me. When he heard Roberto yell, he ran to get the emergency workers.

Officer Fields and I make a good team. I find the lost person. I bark. Then Officer Fields takes over. He knows just what to do.

The emergency workers rushed over. They carefully moved the rubble. It was slow work. They didn't want a piece of wood or wall to hit Roberto.

Officer Fields and I watched as the pile became smaller and smaller. Then I saw the best thing I had seen all day.

Roberto's face poked out from the pile. He was dirty, but he was smiling!

Officer Fields patted my head. "Good work, boy!" he said to me. "Now let's hope Roberto isn't hurt."

Chapter 7
Lucky, Lucky Roberto

The emergency workers freed Roberto. He was a very lucky boy. He had been trapped in a small space under a piece of a wall. He couldn't get out. However, nothing else could fall on him and hurt him.

Roberto wanted to jump up on his own. The emergency workers did not like that at all.

They told Roberto to stay still. They said they would take him out on a stretcher. Then he would have to go to the hospital for a checkup.

The emergency workers put Roberto on a stretcher. Officer Fields and I followed as they carried him to an ambulance.

Suddenly, a woman rushed up to Officer Fields. She looked very worried. I figured she was Roberto's mother. I was right.

"Where's my boy?" she screamed.

"I'm OK, Mom," Roberto said. "I'm safe now, thanks to Officer Fields and Champ. I could hear Champ barking. That's when I knew to yell for help."

Roberto's mother looked over at Officer
Fields. She shook hands with him and thanked
him. Then she reached down and scratched me
behind the ears just like Roberto had done.

Officer Fields looked serious. I knew he had a few questions to ask Roberto.

Chapter 8
Best Friends for Life

"Roberto," he said, "what made you leave the hallway at such a dangerous time? Why did you run back to the classroom?"

Roberto looked embarrassed. "I know what I did was not very smart," he said. "But I left my picture of you and Champ in the classroom. I didn't want to lose it. So I went back to get it."

Officer Fields scolded Roberto a little bit. He made him promise he would never run away again in an emergency.

Then he became his old friendly self. "I'm glad you're safe," he said. "And I'll make sure you get another picture." We watched the emergency workers put Roberto in the ambulance. His mother got in beside him.

"Looks like our work is done," Officer
Fields said to me.

Before we got back into our car, an emergency worker ran back to us. He said Roberto wanted me to ride in the ambulance, too!

I looked up at Officer Fields.

"Go ahead, boy," he said. "I'll follow along in the car. I'll pick you up at the hospital."

I ran over to the ambulance and hopped in.

Roberto smiled when I got in. His mother
smiled, too. I sat down next to Roberto and
gently put my head in his lap.

"It looks like you have a friend," Roberto's
mom said.

"That's right," Roberto said, "a friend for
life."

Glossary

ambulance (AM byuh luns) a special truck that has medical supplies and equipment and is used for taking sick or injured people to a hospital

drill (drihl) an activity that is repeated over and over again to make people ready for an emergency

emergency (ee MUR jun see) surprise event that needs immediate attention

muggy (MUG ee) weather that is warm and damp, but not raining

pressure (PRESH ur) the force of something pushing down on something else

rescue (RES kyoo) to save someone or something from danger

rubble (RUB ul) rock or concrete broken into small pieces

stretcher (STRECH ur) a piece of canvas or cloth attached to a frame that is used to carry an injured person

temperature (TEM pur uh chur) how hot or cold something or someone is

tornado (tor NAY doh) a column of wind that comes from a thundercloud and turns violently